Hire Train Monitor Motivate

Build Wealth with Common Stocks

The Ten Domains of Effective Goal Setting

Hire Train Monitor Motivate

Build an Organization, Team, or Career of Distinction in the Transformational Workplace

David J. Waldron

Country View

To Suzan: for your love and for building a home of distinction.

CONTENTS ▌

*H*ire *Train Monitor Motivate* is the culmination of more than two decades of learning and practicing organizational leadership, team management, and individual performance in the transformational workplace. I began formalizing the principles around the year 2005 and used it as a template for a career training business that we built from about 350 customers to over 1,000—and 40 employees to over 100—in five years. Despite the rapid growth, the institution enjoyed a strong compliance record, including zero findings of noncompliance during several third-party quality assurance reviews.

During this time frame, I was given an opportunity to present the concepts of *Hire Train Monitor Motivate* at a companywide meeting of the organization's team builders. Several years later, an attendee at the original meeting was celebrated as the company's leader of the year. As I was congratulating her, she offered that my presentation was an inspiration for her performance and had applied the principles of *Hire Train Monitor Motivate* during her team's rise to award-winning status. I was humbled as much as honored. From that moment, I was inspired to share these concepts with professionals interested in building organizations, teams, and individual careers of distinction and whose performance or perceptions might benefit as a result.

My goal is to present *Hire Train Monitor Motivate* as a catalyst, a blueprint of organizational, team, and individual effectiveness in the twenty-first century local and global workplaces. My professional memoir as a proud veteran leader of organizations where motivated stakeholders learn and earn from the benefits of building or contributing to teams and individuals of distinction.

In this spirit, the seven chapters of *Hire Train Monitor Motivate* strive to offer a simple yet inspiring template for organizations, teams, and individual contributors seeking to achieve or sustain a high quality and financially stable operation. Groups focused on the desired ethical outcomes of customers, colleagues, and other principal stakeholders.

Chapter One: First People, Then Vision presents a classic paradox in organizational effectiveness, first conveyed by author Jim Collins in his classic, *Good to Great*. Collins's book was the primary inspiration during my leadership of several award-winning organizations and teams. Included in Chapter One are the four character traits I have found universal among productive employees and entrepreneurs.

Chapter Two: Build an Organization, Team, or Career of Distinction, examines strategies to nurture a company, group, or individual toward excellence in a customer-centric environment. Chapter Three: Master the Art of Workplace Transformation assesses how to generate organizational quality from an employee-driven culture by focusing daily on the learned art of hiring for optimism, training for quality, monitoring for compliance, and motivating for performance.

Because most organization members are team players and not leaders, the emphasis in Chapter Three—and throughout the book—is on individual career effectiveness. In other words, how the reader presents him or herself in the workplace as someone hired and retained for a positive attitude, trained for a commitment to quality, monitored for dedication to compliance, and motivated to perform at or above expectations.

Chapter Four: Play the Game the Right Way provides an operational model with a history of delivering outstanding organization, team, and individual outcomes by embracing the six cultural realities essential for the long-term sustainability of an institution of commerce. Chapter Five: Leadership and Teamwork by Inclusion speaks to balancing the demands of seven interested participants in a typical organization by first adopting a leadership or teamwork model of inclusion, then driving an economic model of mutually dependent engines.

Chapter Six: Make Your Workplace a Great Place identifies paradigms to career achievement for each stakeholder's benefit. Included in this section are suggested practical rules to implement at the organization, team, and individual levels, plus how to confront the challenging aspects of being a role model or other active participant in the so-called sharing economy of today's ever-expanding local and global marketplaces.

Hire Train Monitor Motivate concludes with Chapter Seven: Your Essential Role in the Transformational Workplace by presenting several concepts, including the Millennial Model, that redefine critical roles necessary to remain an active participant in the twenty-first century local and global economies.

For brevity, references to *customers* throughout the book indicate any individual or group served by an organization, team, employee, or sole proprietor. Included are clients, patients, constituents, readers, viewers, students, parents, visitors, diners, purchasers, buyers, patrons, borrowers, shoppers, taxpayers, consumers, and so forth. In other words, how an organization—whether in the for-profit, nonprofit, or public domain—designates the ultimate beneficiary of its goods or services.

References to *leadership* in the book, whether implied or expressed, speak to individuals—regardless of position or rank—that are engaged in improving an organization, team, or individual career.

* * *

Several outstanding mentors, peers, and protégés influenced my rewarding career in organizational development, team building, and personal career effectiveness. Partners of distinction to whom I owe my sincerest gratitude for making a lasting impact on my performance; and, of most importance, for contributing to the positive outcomes of thousands of customers and hundreds of colleagues.

I dedicate this book to each influential partner, every passionate, caring organization or team member serving and supporting customers whose lives are improving each day from the hiring, training, monitoring, and motivating individual careers of distinction in the local and global economies.

Thank you, the reader, for investing valuable resources into this book and for your tireless and passionate contributions to the noble and worthy mission of your transformational workplace.

David J. Waldron, Author

Hire Train Monitor Motivate

First People, Then Vision

Organizations, teams, and individuals of distinction that have mastered the art of workplace effectiveness exhibit a mutual characteristic of putting people first, thus empowering a collective discovery of the mission, vision, and values of the group's culture.

In his seminal book, *Good to Great* (Harper Business),[1] Jim Collins offers a classic illustration of placing people before vision. Collins and his research team studied organizations that transformed from mere good companies to great, legendary enterprises. The team found several common denominators in the companies studied, and many of the shared traits were paradoxical to conventional wisdom.

His book's initial concept is perhaps the most contradictory of Collins's conclusions. He found great organizations first hired the best talent each could find and afford and then allowed those individuals to determine the organization's vision and mission. In other words, let capable people create the culture of the company. Collins translated his notion into a believable concept by asking, "First who, then what?"

* * *

[1]*GOOD TO GREAT – Why Some Companies Make the Leap...and Others Don't*. Copyright © 2001 by Jim Collins. Published by Harper Business (an imprint of HarperCollins Publishers, Inc.) For more information, visit jimcollins.com. Reprinted with permission of Curtis Brown, Ltd.

People Drive the Culture

One may find it difficult to argue against Collins's academic theory, supported by empirical evidence that suggests teams of collaborative individuals drive an organization's culture.

Nonetheless, it is rare to find such a compelling and counterintuitive paradigm in today's workplace. More often, a small group of owners or executives at the top set the vision and then seek talent to fit into a culture defined by those values. But does this conventional wisdom of placing vision before people work?

To test the typical strategy first, people second culture found in many organizations today, ask a well-regarded employee or coworker what he or she thinks of your organization's mission and culture. Political correctness notwithstanding, you may expect a flattering, albeit brief, and to the point answer. Then ask what they would add or delete from the published vision, mission, and values statements. I guarantee the time he or she spends answering your follow-up question far exceeds the former. The concept of people first is manifested as motivated employees prefer to be a harbinger of the vision instead of a mere follower.

But how do you find outstanding, self-disciplined staff or become one?

Interview for Greatness

I have long observed the second you need to micromanage someone, you have made a hiring mistake. Overcome this common workplace dilemma by hiring, referring, or becoming a disciplined, talented, and committed individual of distinction. Treat any required credentials as secondary to first screening candidates—or your performance—for self-discipline, demonstrated capability, and an unyielding commitment to workplace excellence.

To illustrate a real-world example of putting discipline, talent, and commitment ahead of credentials, I once ran a career college where I had stopped counting how many students had expressed to me that a particular faculty member was the best teacher ever, going back to kindergarten. This coveted instructor was a disciplinarian that maintained classroom control, although she taught in a kind, dedicated, and thoughtful manner. Students respected her for the consistency. She was a born teacher, yet never took her natural talent for granted, working hard and going above and beyond for her students without letting any off the hook. In the eyes of students, peers, and administrators, she was the best.

Nevertheless, while pursuing the more desirable regional accreditation to replace our national accreditation, and although the instructor had a bachelor's degree from an Ivy League university in the subject matter taught, the accreditation visiting team determined that she was not eligible to teach specific courses. Her master's degree was not in the field as required by the standards. The best teacher ever yet lacked the right credential. I wanted to give a copy of *Good to Great* to each member of the accreditation team.

Four Common Traits of Successful Team Members

Although by no surprise, this same great instructor displayed four personality traits that I found as a hiring manager often predict the success or failure of individuals in an organization or team setting.

- Assertive: a values-driven communicator.
- Self-directed: performs with limited or no supervision.
- Other-directed: demonstrates a genuine customer focus.
- Work ethic: exhibits dedication and character.

Two immutable facts about the four traits of a successful team member are 1) the employee must own all four with significance, and 2) the qualities must be discovered in the hiring process because the four traits, for the most part, are not trainable.

Assertive does not mean aggressive. Ethical, confident associates demonstrate a substantial capacity for communicating well with a focus on values and problem-solving. During the formal interview, ask the candidate to share how they identified and solved a pressing problem in the workplace. The answer may demonstrate appropriate assertiveness or lack thereof.

Next, take the applicant on a tour of the store, shop, factory, warehouse, clinic, or office suite as an opportunity to observe his or her interactions with staff, customers, and vendors. Thriving businesses or nonprofit organizations—including those operating in challenging and competitive markets—require employees with ethical assertiveness.

Self-directed—also denoted as self-motivated—depicts the team member's discipline when left with limited supervision. Do not ask the candidate direct questions about self-motivation because skillful interviewees—not guaranteed to be good employees—may have prepared answers that he or she assumes you want to hear. Instead, challenge the candidate with questions about specific projects or job duties they were forced to complete independently. Listen to how confident they were in tackling and completing tasks at work, including unpopular experiences.

Other-directed, often described as customer service, has become a dinosaur in commerce today. Nevertheless, avoid confusing this trait with outgoing personalities as a majority of individuals in society, and, therefore, workplaces are extroverted. It's best to have caring and motivated team players—including introverts—who are genuine about taking care of the stakeholder, whether a customer, coworker, owner, donor, manager, vendor, competitor or regulator.

During the hiring process, ask the candidate his or her perception of serving customers and other stakeholders. The answer should equate to: "I love doing this so much; getting paid a fair wage for it is a bonus!"

Work ethic is perhaps the trait most associated with the expression, "You cannot teach that." However, it does involve more than just showing up on time, putting in the necessary effort to complete the job at hand, or being responsible for the workload. Work ethic is more about character and self-discipline.

Being responsible, avoiding impulsive behavior, and taking the high road are common in those with a sound work ethic. Interview questions are simple: "Take me through a typical workday from arrival to departure. Tell me about the last time you were in an unexpected confrontation with a customer or coworker. How did you handle it?" Get to the character of the candidate.

Confident, dynamic, customer-centered employees who demonstrate self-discipline often prevail in successful organizations or teams that embrace performance-driven cultures.

Interview for greatness by screening your candidates for the four traits of successful team members, i.e., assertive, self-directed, other-directed, and possessing a strong work ethic. And remember to present all four when you are the interviewee.

The Transformational Workplace

Imagine an office, institution, shop, call or data center, factory, warehouse, clinic, or store with a culture that allows employee interrogation of processes? An organization that takes responsibility when things do not go as planned? Leadership that is devoid of having all the answers but engages with questioning to empower instead of stymie? A team that facilitates open dialogue in problem-solving; and investigates issues for resolution instead of culpability?

What if there were no written warnings, no annual performance reviews other than equitable pay increases; no Bible-long rules of conduct; no wrenching restructuring, cost-cutting, or other repressive tactics that paralyze more than stimulate an organization?

Try envisioning department managers or team leaders running the organization instead of the well-intentioned, although sometimes detrimental, legal and human resource departments. Organizations and teams of distinction are magnificent because each first hires and nurtures disciplined, talented, committed professionals. It then allows those individuals to create the group's culture by setting the mission, vision, and values.

Drive Your Economic Engine

During my three decades in the workplace, it became apparent how organizations get sidetracked from the economic mission, often the enterprise's founding purpose.

For any organization, whether for-profit, nonprofit, or in the public service, driving its economic engine is as simple as:

> Adequate new business procurement + quality products or services + ethical practices + high customer satisfaction = a profitable or solvent enterprise.

Regardless of the chosen formula for success, there is no room for predatory sales, devalued cost structures, unethical practices, or minimal standards. On the contrary, it takes a disciplined and caring work environment focused on doing the right thing by hiring and retaining employees who solicit, service, support, and re-engage qualified customers to the direct advantage of each stakeholder. Constituents that benefit include the customer, employee, shareholder, donor, taxpayer, vendor, regulator, and public.

Understanding and driving your organization or team's economic engine is a fundamental requirement of a successful enterprise. Ignore or compromise your engine, and it may seize.

What is Your Organization or Team the Best At?

A question that was a central theme for the great companies in Jim Collins's research was, "What is your organization the best in the world at?" Successful companies want to know the one big audacious thing the organization can understand and be committed to. What does the team employ as its core solution to competitive threats and changes in the industry? What must you be passionate about, best in the world, and make a profit or surplus by doing?

I challenge readers to engage their colleagues by asking the question, "What are or can we be the best in the world at?" You may be amazed by the passionate contributions to this exercise.

For example, at a career school that I led as campus president, we decided to hire top talent and often asked the best in the world question. The consensus was *event management*, demonstrated by willing participation throughout the faculty, staff, and administration ranks.

The improvements in student enrollment, retention, and job placement, capped by a spectacular graduation ceremony from this joint effort in event planning and execution, were significant. We became known as the company's preeminent campus for event management expertise and were soon contacted by other locations nationwide for our best practices.

* * *

First people, then vision puts great players on the team bus that lead it on a successful journey determined to benefit customers and other interested stakeholders. Emphasis is placed on the journey instead of the destination, as a voyage of greatness may endure far beyond any finite endpoint.

You, your team, and your organization deserve to be on a journey of distinction. Be committed first to hire—or refer—and then retain the best personnel possible, i.e., employees or coworkers that are assertive, self-directed, customer-focused, and have a strong work ethic.

Drive a culture of discipline, talent, and commitment, in a caring way. Be a champion of organization, team, and individual transformation in your workplace. Remain forever focused on your economic engine. Discover what you, your coworkers, and your organization do well, and then be the best in the world at it.

Two

Build an Organization, Team or Career of Distinction

It is essential to operate—or participate—in a customer-centric organization, team, or individual career without compromising the needs of other stakeholders, such as owners or donors; senior management or administrators; coworkers; vendors; and regulators. A consensus-driven culture of teamwork, performance, compliance, and recognition—centered on the desired customer and other stakeholder outcomes—forms the foundation for an organization, team, or career of distinction.

Teamwork: Getting Along

Building consensus begins with collaboration. As discussed in Chapter One, First People, Then Vision, hire the most disciplined and committed team players available, then empower that talent to partner in creating the organization's mission, vision, values, and culture. Incorporate definitive ways of developing or contributing to teams driven by accord; groups that enjoy working together to be the best in the world at the goods and services it produces.

I have observed that the most productive teams debate or argue over policies, ideas, or customer welfare. It is because of those involved care. Compassion is an essential ingredient for building and sustaining success in a cohesive team environment.

Consensus building is challenging among self-interested departments, sometimes labeled as silos. Well-managed organizations break down silos by encouraging cooperation that often spreads throughout the ranks among department leaders.

Facilitating regular communication between departments or teams is another key to building consensus. Unless already doing so, contribute—as you deem appropriate based on your workplace culture—to influence these engagements in motivating, productive, and measurable ways.

Staff meetings play a significant role in team building despite the universal perception as a meager use of time. Therefore, ensure each scheduled get-together has a published agenda, is brief, productive, fixated on a consensus, and is outcomes-driven.

As a rule, consensus-building starts at the top with the organization's president or department director in partnership with team leaders. Management that promotes openness, constructive feedback, visibility, and trust, builds teams united for the betterment of its customers and all interested stakeholders.

Performance: Getting It Done

I have never worked in or observed a successful organization or team that was not performance-driven. Excellent team and individual outcomes, consistent customer satisfaction, robust regulatory and legal compliance, beneficial shareholder or donor returns, and workplace fulfilled staff is the order of any sustainable organization, team, or career of distinction.

Helping customers and making the numbers must coexist for any motivated organization, team, or individual to succeed in today's competitive local and global workplaces.

Depending on the employee's personality, people-focused or numbers-driven, heads spin from the sheer volume of workplace responsibilities. Today's typical work environment requires an individual or team's ability to keep several balls in the air at once.

Amid the essential customer activity, organizations, teams, and individuals are committed to sustaining institutional effectiveness. The parallel focus is on quality standards, government regulations, administrative capability, employee recruitment and training; human resource policy; facilities management; information technology infrastructure; workplace safety and security, legal disputes, and corporate reporting requirements. Not to mention the ever-expected, although sometimes unexpected, interruption or surprise. It is never-ending.

A thriving operation is a haven of individuals and numbers, driven by outcomes. It is not for the faint of heart. It takes a capacity for empathy, resilience, and emotional intelligence to navigate and survive an atmosphere fixated on the team or individual's performance.

When the going gets tough, do what you do best. Follow-up with a customer, refer a new employee, submit a cost-saving idea, solve a problem, or help a colleague. If, as a result, you are drained of emotion, practice work/life balance and take approved time off. It is the cure for what ails you in the performance-driven, twenty-first century workplace.

Although, upon returning to the store, shop, factory, warehouse, call center, clinic, institution, or office, you may be reminded that efforts are not confused with results. It is about getting it done and done right.

Compliance: Getting It Right

In recent years, growing numbers of industries have placed a renewed emphasis on regulatory compliance. Perplexing are ethics, adherence to regulations, and playing the game right have always been paramount to the survival of organizations, teams, and individual careers in the local or global marketplaces.

The compelling reason for the enduring and ever-increasing regulatory oversight from international, federal, state, and local government agencies are organizations making a profit or surplus from continuing operations. Relevant goods or services are often held as socialistic, i.e., beneficial to consumer well-being or greater public interest within our capitalistic society.

Regardless, it is inexcusable for a company to have the phrase *be ethical* listed as the eleventh commandment on a top ten list of operational priorities, as I once witnessed. You must play the game right more than anyone else. For many industries in the post-Great Recession, the alternative is a death knell.

It is comparable to being hunted. You may run, hide, or play dead, although it is recommended to stand up as accountable in the regulated workplace. Be proud of your accomplishments and commitment to the rules regardless of whether you are one hundred percent in agreement with each.

Think of your organization or team's symbol of regulatory compliance as a four-legged chair: one leg is for international or federal oversight, one is for state or local government, one is for industry standards, and one is for your organization's written policies. A team of distinction works each day to keep all four legs of the compliance chair firm to the ground.

Your customers deserve a commitment to quality. Your staff or colleagues deserve it. Investors, donors, taxpayers, vendors, accreditors, and regulators deserve it. Play the game right and be accountable because you deserve recognition for your devotion to quality and compliance.

Recognition: Getting to Celebrate

When motivating teams and individuals, is there anything more persuasive than formal or informal recognition of performance and notable efforts? Included here are repeated acknowledgments of the accomplishments and struggles of customers and employees.

Although there is a tenet that must be followed with diligence for recognition to become a functional and motivating aspect of any people-intensive operation:

Praise in public. Reprimand in private.

Break the above rule just once with a customer, employee, or coworker, and you will pay. Perhaps, we all have been victims of being praised anonymously in private and reprimanded with an unwanted ceremony in public.

Before applauding or admonishing, remember how it feels, and you will do it right every time. Your organization, team, and career will reap dividends from your kind approach to the everyday workplace habits of often praising in plain view and reprimanding—only when necessary—behind closed doors.

Facilitate recognition by sponsoring awards ceremonies where you celebrate organization, team, and individual accomplishments. Quality plaques inscribed with thoughts of gratitude, consumables such as office supplies, other essential tools of the trade, or gift certificates are worth the effort with nominal expenditures required.

Other examples of praising in public include a convenient parking space for a month; or handwritten notes of thanks shared with the employee and family, coworkers, and friends. Take the team to lunch—include everyone—although single out extraordinary individual performances when addressing the group with the obligatory thank you speech. Erect a wall of fame that displays notable employees or coworkers with pride and his or her written permission. Buy and serve the department or team a meal or a snack.

If budgets permit, contemplate hiring a motivational speaker that colleagues will connect with instead of your public relations department's politically motivated choice. Invest in your team meetings. Hold each gathering in a high-profile, convenient location. Decorate the event with class and dignity. Use current technology. Celebrate achievements.

And if your chief financial officer or business manager questions the line item merits of your morale-boosting budgeted expenditures, ask with politeness what he or she suggests as an alternative.

Whether honoring customers, colleagues, or the families of each, celebrate success. Be creative. Be thankful. Be sincere. Be compliant. Do it in public. Do it often. I guarantee you are renowned for your zeal to acknowledge successful efforts and compassionate contributions.

Quality Reflects a Customer-Centric Climate

Corporate and regional managers; accreditors; and regulators that visit multiple organizations as part of regular job responsibilities have often shared that when entering a workplace, they can either cut the tension in the air with a knife or sense an aura of positive energy and professionalism. How does a visitor to your workplace—whether virtual or online—describe its kinesthetic atmosphere?

The principles discussed throughout *Hire Train Monitor Motivate* are about creating a team or workplace that exudes a collaborative, positive, and ethical customer-centric culture; a haven of mutual trust, dignity, and respect; along with shared enthusiasm for working together on a joint mission.

Partnering as a team by getting along, driving performance by getting it done, being compliant by doing it right, and remembering to distinguish your efforts by celebrating success, are paramount to pride and performance in thriving organizations. These are the common traits found in high-achieving teams and individuals that have mastered the art of workplace effectiveness. Because each settles for nothing short of what colleagues work for and customers pay for: to create and maintain quality goods and services produced and delivered by organizations, teams, and individuals of distinction.

Three

Master the Art of Workplace Transformation

C ustomer-centered, teamwork-focused, and consensus-driven organizations share a commitment to excellence in the recruitment and retention of employees that duly serve their constituents. The unending responsibility is to hire, train, monitor, and motivate passionate contributors focused on the desired customer and organizational outcomes.

I was fortunate to serve successful tenures in institutional leadership and team building by learning and practicing the art of hiring, training, monitoring, and motivating. These four skills are necessary, in unison, to build and maintain an organization, team, or individual career of distinction.

HIRE FOR OPTIMISM

As discussed in Chapter One: First People, Then Vision, and Chapter Two: Build an Organization, Team, or Career of Distinction, hiring—or referring—the best talent possible and practicing successful career management is paramount. Nonetheless, this productive recruiting method is counterintuitive to the conventional approach of focusing on qualifications and technical skills in the credential-obsessed workplaces of today's competitive marketplaces.

The key is to expand your search beyond the required checks and balances of matching candidates to the department or corporate human resource requirements. Build a team of greatness by hiring or referring qualified individuals with optimistic mindsets. Or maintain an attitude of distinction as an individual contributor. In either case, the fuel is provided for a winning team.

The Group Interview Revisited

Contemplate a different approach to group interviews. Turn the table by first presenting your organization or department and its employment opportunity in a professional and entertaining format. Then allow your guests to sneak out of the building during a scheduled break if he or she determines the job or culture is not suitable. No hard feelings as you let everyone know in your opening statement that it is okay to exit with grace. The department and organization wish everyone great success in their future career endeavors.

As far as the candidates that choose to return from the intermission, rest assured you have the undivided attention of those individuals.

Now have each participant share with the entire group why he or she is the best candidate for the job opportunity presented and, therefore, deserves a scheduled formal interview. Then ask each candidate to vote for their choice in anonymity—it cannot be him or her—including a brief narrative on why. You may be amazed by the results.

If you are not a hiring manager, refer candidates to the group seminar, or volunteer to assist in the festivities. I guarantee you experience joy from the fruits of your labor in contributing to your organization or team's building.

I have hired some of my best employees from group interviews. The cream rises to the top. The winners often emerge at the starting gate.

Turn the Table in the One-on-One Interview

As an alternative, use the same presentation and approach as the group interview to present the job opening in the one-on-one interview. In the opening statement, grant the candidate permission to end the meeting at any time if the opportunity is not as envisioned. When choosing to remain, as a majority often does in the individual format, have the interviewee explain at the close why he or she is the best fit for the job. Invite back those that impress for a second, more formal interview.

Once hired, the most dedicated employees sometimes submit a letter of resignation because a once-in-a-lifetime opportunity found him or her that you were unable to match, or perhaps there is an unexpected spouse or partner relocation. Surprises such as these are why you need to be interviewing in regular intervals, regardless of openings. Put more memorably:

Maintain blue suits in the lobby.

Employees Join Organizations and Leave Managers

It is often said or witnessed that selected candidates join organizations with enthusiasm and then leave managers or supervisors with disdain. Be inquisitive in vetting the potential future supervisors and coworkers to whom you are interviewing to the same degree you hold the organization.

When hiring or referring, be bold and confident and allow the candidate as much access to the supervisors or coworkers as is reasonable. This vetting process may eliminate the common ailment of good employees leaving bad managers after joining an organization or vice versa.

* * *

Recruit or refer new hires that possess genuine positive attitudes at the starting gate and perhaps never worry again about colleagues sprouting negative outlooks in your workplace. Optimistic minds produce positive results that create great places to work.

TRAIN FOR QUALITY

I have found that a universal response from employee surveys is the perceived need for additional training. We are learning creatures and have a perennial openness to further instruction, regardless of the level already offered. Therefore, whether a facilitator or a learner, it is essential to remain in perpetual training mode.

Nonetheless, any employee training program needs to focus on technical and regulatory requirements, in addition to personal and group performances toward the expected organizational, team, and individual outcomes.

First Impressions are Forever

Orientations are important onboarding events for new employees. The old cliché, "first impressions are lasting," endures. It is recommended to have formal full-day new employee orientations with a written, segued agenda including interdepartmental participation. And as soon as the new employee completes the required human resources paperwork, set him or her on a day to remember.

Include an impassioned tour of relevant information and introductions. Take him or her to lunch. At the end of the orientation, leave the new employee thinking, "This is the best first day of work, ever!"

Individual vs. Group Training

Group training sessions are often fun and productive for the non-sales departments. Sales and marketing teams enjoy group enlightenment as well, although, in my experience, salespeople are susceptible to picking up bad habits in group learning paradigms. Contemplate limiting sales personnel to individual training sessions with his or her supervisor.

Nevertheless, train for quality performance. Time constraints aside, learning opportunities are productive vehicles for communicating goals and measuring outcomes that teams and individuals have committed to achieving, as well as an excellent opportunity to praise in public.

Hire talented, qualified players and training sessions become rewarding get-togethers that celebrate success; a guaranteed welcomed alternative to forced learning where employees come to regret checking "more training, please" on the survey in the first place.

Regardless of how presented, when participants perceive the training as a celebration of effort and an opportunity to learn things unknown, gatherings become popular events that inspire performance because of it as opposed to despite it.

Ninety-Day Impact

Whether hiring and training or being hired and trained, performance during the first ninety days on a new job or promotion often dictates the employee's long-term contributions, for better or worse.

As the hiring or training manager, be aware of the recruit's behavior, commitment, motivation, and desire to succeed during this critical learning period. If you are the recruit, have a plan of action to gain as much knowledge of the job description as possible, and then demonstrate a command of the new position. Remind yourself each day that what you accomplish during the first ninety days will leave a lasting impression on your supervisor and coworkers.

An excellent way to measure new employee success, including your own, is to make a difference right from the starting gate. Initial ninety-day evaluations are a useful tool in determining the success of the hiring process and training regimen. Was the hire a good match? If yes, did the orientation and training programs set the new employee on a path to long-term success?

Think of the ninety-day impact as similar in scope to the first one hundred days in the White House for a new president of the United States. Political wisdom says what the president accomplishes in his or her first one hundred days in office more often defines the president's legacy.

Authenticate your potential long-term contributions to your new job or your recruit's performance by delivering or observing the ninety-day impact. An extraordinary one hundred days are okay, too.

* * *

Onboard your new employees or coworkers with robust orientation programs that lead to positive first impressions. Train new and veteran employees for quality and be open to new ideas and ways of supporting the development and manufacture of your organization's products or services.

Observe performance during the first ninety days on the job to measure long-term potential and whether the new employee, perhaps yourself included, is a good fit. Your customers and, as a positive consequence, the organization's stakeholders will benefit from the commitment to excellence.

MONITOR FOR COMPLIANCE

Contrary to conventional wisdom or political meandering, significant regulatory compliance issues in today's workplaces result from negligence and under sight, more so than intent. Therefore, a compliance monitoring program designed and implemented to support and protect employees may be more productive than if presented—or perceived—as a mere defense of the organization's stock price or reputation.

Get It Right or Game Over

Monitoring for compliance involves assisting staff in understanding and appreciating the myriad of government regulations, industry standards, and the organization or team's written policies, criteria that forever loom over an individual contributor. Employees often share, or think, what is *not known* is of utmost concern.

Preference is to focus on learning what is unknown in a culture of trust and understanding. Mystery shops, corporate visits, and other compliance monitoring become expected daily activities—not surprises—toward a squeaky clean, ethical and vibrant workplace.

Reward adherence to compliance in public, and coach shortcomings, in private. Thus, make it part of the culture, thus eliminating the proverbial skeletons in the closet or eight hundred pound gorilla in the room.

When It's Everyone's Responsibility—It's No One's

Why do some organizations insist on employing sales directors, department managers, financial talent, engineers, customer service representatives, designers, fundraisers, technicians, and so forth, but not regulatory compliance directors? Assuming the team leader is the director of compliance by default is a fiscal cop-out. The notion of regulatory conformance as everyone's responsibility is also doomed to failure.

When everyone is in charge, no one is in charge.

To illustrate the power of a director of compliance at the local level, I once employed a gentleman in that role after being named the president of a degree-granting career school. He earned his annual salary early on by discovering two regulatory facts about our institution overlooked for decades.

The school was not subject to its then oversight by an onerous state regulatory agency whose purview was non-degree-granting schools. And, as an accredited degree-granting institution, we had the authority to use the word "college" in our name, thought impossible under previous corporate and campus interpretations of state legislation and regulations.

When we asked state officials why these two profound regulatory realities were not already in place, the frank answer was: "Because nobody ever challenged either, no one ever asked." After filling out a few forms and recording a sworn statement, we were granted college status under the state's higher education body's authority that oversaw the traditional public and private colleges, including several world-renowned research universities.

Last I heard, the industrious director of compliance was working his expertise at an Ivy League school. Well done and deserved.

* * *

Monitor for regulatory compliance or support your organization's formal observation of you and your colleagues' relevant daily activities. Make it a priority. Make it fun. But do it. The organization, its customers, and other stakeholders are counting on your due diligence.

* * *

MOTIVATE FOR PERFORMANCE

I am a certified practitioner in the behavioral science of neuro-linguistic programming (NLP) and submit its principles are terrific resources for motivating or staying motivated in an ethical workplace. NLP—first developed in the 1970s by Richard Bandler and John Grinder—presents a blackboard of outstanding communication techniques suited to the transformational workplace.

For brevity, I offer, here, a few select presuppositions or premises that—when understood and practiced—may go a long way toward significant improvement in the motivation of teams and individuals of distinction.

There are Two Persons in Everyone

NLP theory works from the premise that each of us communicates to the world via our conscious and subconscious minds.

Our conscious mind attempts to justify our thought processes, decision-making, and oral and written communications. We tend to motivate—or stay motivated—in the workplace based on our conscious state of mind's rational thought and behavior. In contrast, our subconscious mind taps our brain's database of a lifetime of learned values, beliefs, and motives, as well as our intuitive experience of the world around us and the future ahead of us.

To be effective in the ethical persuasion or motivation of a team member, you must be aware of that individual's conscious and subconscious thoughts.

For example, a team member operating from a conscious state of mind may declare an enthusiastic buy-in to the new strategic initiative.

But on a subconscious level, they have undeclared doubts about the proposal based on past negative experiences similar to the plan's parameters. In this instance, the conscious mind is compelled toward the political correctness of buying-in as the subconscious contemplates potential objections and ramifications that may surface—without expectation—at a later date.

Consequently, how do you distinguish between these two states of mind without being patronizing?

Motivate Via the Three Sensory Channels

There are limited substitutes for the three primary sensory channels of communication most familiar to the workplace: visual, auditory, and kinesthetic. In all due respect to readers in the foodservice industry that uses the gustatory, or taste channel, and several other professions that enlist the olfactory—or smell channel—or perhaps the sense of touch; the focus here is on the three ordinary senses of sight, hearing, and emotional feeling.

I have found no better vehicle for understanding staff and colleagues' motivations than to be aware of how they communicate in the workplace via their sensory channels.

It is presumed—any physical disabilities notwithstanding—that each of us communicates from a place of visual, auditory, and kinesthetic paths, yet, as a unique individual, we are dominant in one of the three. At a minimum, you should decipher an individual's sequential use of the three channels in everyday oral and written communications.

Listen to or read the colleague's use of words. You may find predominance in a single channel.

- Visual Person: "I *see* what you mean. Let's take a *look* at the report."
- Auditory Person: "I *hear* you on that issue. Let's *listen* to what she has to *say*."

- Kinesthetic Person: "I am getting the *sense* things are going to change for the better. The new team member has a *warm* personality. I do *feel* good about partnering with him on the project."

The above examples demonstrate how simple it is to determine an individual's dominant communication channel by taking inventory of predominant keywords. Once you are comfortable understanding their prevailing sensory channel, remember to communicate with the colleague in that path through simple word choices, whether spoken or written. As a result, they may feel connected to your dialogue at a conscious or subconscious level.

Here are sample matching responses that correspond to the previous examples.

- Visual Person: "I *see* what you mean. Let's take a *look* at the report."
  - Your matching response: "Okay, and the good news is the info is easy to *visualize*."
- Auditory Person: "I *hear* you on that issue. Let's *listen* to what she has to *say*."
  - Your matching response: "*Sounds* like a plan!"
- Kinesthetic Person: "I am getting the *sense* things are going to change for the better. The new team member has a *warm* personality. I do *feel* good about partnering with him on the project."
  - Your matching response: "I understand his former team gave him a *heartfelt* sendoff."

Matching and translating someone's predominant communication style is a basic NLP premise in the art of motivating for performance. We perhaps all know someone superb at connecting with people, making fast friends, or influencing others. I submit that an individual's ability to motivate via the three sensory channels is anchored in the theoretical knowledge of the NLP hypothesis of these paths of interaction, if not from a predisposition or intuitive connection to the concept.

Effective communication and motivation are not limited to the sensory channels. Neuro-linguistic programming concepts run the gamut of several interactive opportunities in the ethical workplace.

The Intent and Response are Independent

The counterintuitive theory behind NLP reasons that any resistance to communication or an idea often reflects the communicator's inflexibility instead of the directive's receiver.

When working with a staff member or a coworker, do not assume any resistance to your communication by them is non-negotiable or a mere stubborn response. First, presume your communication, regardless of form, failed in its desired intent to influence your staff member, coworker, or supervisor. Therefore, you must take responsibility by re-engaging—without defense mechanisms—to persuade your audience to your point of view.

Start by deciphering his or her dominant sensory channel. Is it visual, auditory, or kinesthetic? Isolate the predominant channel and then redesign and deliver the communication by matching and translating your audience's map instead of your territory.

Individuals have the resources necessary to make desired changes in how he or she communicates and motivates. Use this concept to your ethical advantage in achieving your professional or occupational goals. Be responsible for your side of the communication, as that is the only place where you have control. Analyze your message and then improve upon it. On a subconscious level, colleagues may *get* that you take responsibility for your actions to everyone's benefit.

Every Behavior Has a Positive Intent

I suggest that a fundamental NLP presupposition has become more relevant in the dog eat dog workplace of today's so-called sharing economy:

> The positive worth of an individual is held constant as we question the value and appropriateness of internal and external behaviors.

A classic example of the theory of positive intent is that nobody smokes cigarettes because they want to become addicted to nicotine or develop cancer. Positive outcomes such as relaxation, oral fixation, or keeping nervous fingers comfortable may lead to a reliance on smoking.

On the job, a coworker's questionable behaviors that are born of positive intent may include being time and again late for work because of a child's special needs instead of poor work habits. Perhaps a colleague is over contributing during meetings in a vain attempt at winning acceptance from the group more than a mere dominance of it. Another example is a staff member's job-hopping or incessant applications to internal postings, which are not out of the need to improve career opportunities selfishly, but an underlying conscious desire for change and the emotional excitement it brings.

The Winning Approach to Self-Motivation

Staying motivated in your job and career is just as important as inspiring others. A compelling tenet of NLP dictates that an individual more often reaches their goals when moving *towards* the new objective instead of *away* from something where interest has waned.

A prime example of this counterintuitive approach to self-motivation is leaving an organization or team because of frustration with the culture or a supervisor. In this instance, it is critical to redirect your energy towards the potential new opportunities sought and not with the primary aim of leaving the organization.

Productive, self-motivated professionals look forward and move ahead. Unsuccessful self-saboteurs get stuck in the emotions of the departure. Refocus in the direction of your new goal after deciding to end a previous objective, and you may find yourself winning more often in life.

* * *

Consider applying the interactive tools derived from classic NLP modeling. The willingness and ability to motivate—or stay motivated—in ethical ways remain critical to sustaining the roles of organizations, teams, and individual careers in the progressive workplaces of the twenty-first century.

Best Practices in Motivation

Although necessary, one may argue motivating for performance is challenging in today's typical workplace environment. Whether as a team leader or contributor, your attention needs to center on influencing others and remaining motivated in the competitive local and global marketplaces.

Here are ten best practices that ethical, high achieving team leaders are implementing to keep themselves and staff inspired:

1. Catered lunch when the entire team wins.
2. Award ceremonies with approved plaques and giveaways.
3. Fun games for fueling the competitive spirit.
4. Frequent publication of privacy cleared customer, employee, and organizational outcomes to sustain excitement about daily contributions.

5. Require staff attendance at the organization or team meetings that include ceremonies to experience the meaning and ultimate joy of their work.

6. High achieving contributors as speakers, at the heart of the meeting agenda.

7. Publish and distribute privacy cleared lists of honored customers or colleagues for staff to congratulate.

8. Schedule events outside of the primary workplace to engage with the public by promoting what you do well.

9. Conduct customer surveys to correct common denominator issues and share with staff and corporate the positive things customers say about the team and its dedicated players.

10. Remember to praise in public and reprimand in private.

* * *

Motivate, or stay motivated by remaining open to new and ethical communication vehicles, such as the behavioral science of neuro-linguistic programming. At the minimum, employ best practices that keep you, the organization, and its stakeholders excited about the ultimate mission and values that your products or services contribute to the betterment of the local or global marketplaces. Just as important, practice ethical motivational strategies that contribute to a fun and productive workplace of distinction.

Hire, Train, Monitor, and Motivate for Results

By putting stakeholders first—customers in particular—a team or organization is more apt to assimilate to a culture that hires employees for optimistic attitudes in addition to the required credentials. When there are no openings, a constant stream of blue suits from the lobby are interviewed to maintain bench strength. If you are currently seeking new opportunities, then be that blue suit in another organization or team's lobby.

Train for quality, starting with a world-class new employee orientation day, keeping in mind that training is an individual exercise as much as a group activity. Monitor for compliance with laws, regulations, industry standards, and organizational policies in a non-threatening manner. Share a commitment to following the rules by first knowing what the rules are.

Motivate for performance by utilizing the time-tested neuro-linguistic programming techniques and other prescribed best practices to acknowledge and reinforce employee and customer strengths. And tolerate any shortcomings that are not liabilities of the organization.

Applying these and other time-tested principles with consistency, and being open to receiving them, often leads to successful and ethical outcomes.

Now recite and repeat: "*hire* for optimism, *train* for quality, *monitor* for compliance, *motivate* for performance."

Four

Play the Game the Right Way

A straightforward question for any stakeholder of an organization, whether the owner, donor, senior executive, administrator, supervisor, or staff:

> Assuming genuine interest or need exists in the corresponding products or services and at full market value, do you, or would you, engage friends or loved ones in any of your organization's offerings?

If the answer is a resounding "yes," the remainder of this chapter is a recap of what you already know. Hesitation in answering the question is a call for action.

The successful organization, team, or individual of distinction embraces six cultural realities essential for long-term sustainability:

- New customer acquisition drives the organization.
- Product or service quality defines the organization.
- Collecting receivables make paydays possible.
- Regulatory compliance: do it right or game over.
- Financial stability fuels the organization's economic engine.
- Customer satisfaction is the ultimate report card.

An organization that subscribes to these six mantras at the corporate, administrative, department, team, and individual levels is—as often said in professional baseball—playing the game the right way. Delivering operational excellence across the organization is critical to sheer survival. Although just as in competitive sports, elite performance begins with first understanding and then mastering the fundamentals.

New Customer Acquisition Drives the Organization

At virtually every organization, whether for-profit, nonprofit, or in the public service, nothing happens until somebody buys a product, uses a service, makes a donation, or pays his or her taxes.

Unless the sales or fundraising teams acquire new customers, finance cannot fund a client, engineering cannot improve a product, accounting cannot collect receivables, customer service cannot handle an inquiry, and the executive team cannot manage its budget in real-time. Cost-effective marketing, combined with ethical new or repeat customer sales, drives the organization allowing everyone else to perform the essential work each shows up for: serving the needs of customers and other relevant stakeholders.

Product or Service Quality Defines the Organization

During a media interview upon taking over Apple for the second time, Steve Jobs said his commitment to developing cutting-edge devices placed the product ahead of the process. His emphasis was on the merits of the product and the professionals who developed it instead of corporate process or procedure. Given the infamous products Apple has introduced following that interview in the mid-1990s, Jobs's theory has worked in profound ways.

Because of the myriad of regulations and industry standards that face many organizations today, process-driven teams have become the new standard, thus placing product and service development or improvement on the back burner. Customer acquisition, raising financial capital, regulatory compliance, expense management, accounts receivables, legal adherence, human resource policies, customer retention, and other process directed—albeit necessary—activities may undermine the critical role that quality products or services play in a successful organization or team culture.

The quality of an organization's goods or services directly correlates to its reputation in the community. Merchandise or amenities that are up-to-date and delivered with excellence impresses customers, employees, regulators, and competitors; and breeds positive influence on elected officials, mainstream media, and the public.

Organizations and teams that focus on superior product and service delivery develop exceptional reputations in the marketplace. When the pursuit of product or service excellence is ignored or discounted, troubling times are often close behind. Perhaps the new normal of the competitive local and global economies is putting the quality of goods and services above all else. A consequential positive reinvention of universal consumer perceptions lay in the balance.

Collecting Receivables Make Paydays Possible

Any business or organization, regardless of tax status, relies on collecting receivables for financial survival. Successful accounts receivable activity is the lifeblood of the organization's existence as a sound economic entity.

The accounting team or equivalent is assigned the regulatory and procedural responsibility of collecting and posting receivables. Although, this crucial activity is everyone's business as the collection of receivables *makes paydays possible*. For this reason, each employee or team member of the organization is in some way accountable for collecting receivables. To be sure, processing and posting actual collections are limited to sanctioned personnel; however, other employees are role players by default.

Administrative capability in accounts receivables, combined with ethical collection activity—and satisfied customers—often leads to low bad debt, a revealing financial indicator of a rigorous operation. Participation from all team members at approved levels is a predictive gauge of sound collection processes.

On the contrary, lack of discipline, consistency, or ethics in the collections activity often leads to complacency amongst customers with outstanding accounts.

When confronted with the opportunity to assist in your organization's collection process, think of that customer's well-being and your paycheck. Collecting receivables makes both possible.

Regulatory Compliance: Do It Right or Game Over

"Live by the sword or die by the sword" is an ageless expression anchored in the world of commerce. "He or she that holds the gold makes the rules" is another timeless and relevant axiom.

Demonstrate negligence of laws and regulations, even if not deliberate, and it is *game over* for the guilty organization. Operations that are in noncompliance lay as potential victims to the regulatory death knell. The message is clear: play the game right or stop playing the game.

Regulatory compliance in all its forms—international, federal, state, local, accreditation, industry standards, and an organization's written policies—forever remain in the group's consciousness. To live with the benefits of the rules, you are indoctrinated to play by the rules. It is well defined, and for the most part, not negotiable. The alternative is the proverbial penny-wise yet dollar foolish omission, a usual practice in today's ultra-competitive global sharing economy.

The choice is clear, play by the rules or risk ejection from the game. Questioning non-negotiable laws, regulations, standards, or policies is a fool's game. Following them is an act of outright survival. Treat management or fulfillment of regulatory compliance as a priority of your organization, team, and career. Customers and other stakeholders may benefit from the renewed commitment to playing the game the right way.

Financial Stability Fuels the Economic Engine

Meeting or exceeding reasonable financial goals is the lifeblood of any organization's economic engine, whether serving as a for-profit, non-profit, or in the public service.

The team of distinction surpasses the metric goals of current and continuing operations from a myriad of financial commitments. Examples include contributing to research and development, funding marketing plans, paying for the cost of goods sold, hiring and training new talent, capitalizing facilities and equipment, meeting payroll, paying down debt, or making interest payments.

I sometimes observe those in the nonprofit or public service sectors ignore financial scrutiny because of the nonprofit status. Still, not-for-profit translates to tax-exempt status, not an exemption from fiscal responsibility.

And not to take for-profit enterprises off the hook, as excessive profit margins are a call for price reductions to benefit the consumer or investigations of monopolistic or anti-trust violations on behalf of the public as a whole.

Regulatory protection is in peril; due in part to the current divided political landscape epitomized by the post-Great Recession egregious split among voters. This polarizing political reality has lent perilous hands of limiting regulations on the far right and increasing regulatory oversight on the far left.

When such political extremism moderates as heads prevail, rules that benefit all people may give our faltering free-market capitalist structure—which led to the Great Recession—a needed correction to fair market capitalism's balanced economy.

Populist movements may influence a return to the economy of widespread upward mobility for the benefit of future generations of the twenty-first century. Perhaps such action would mirror the legislated re-distribution of excess wealth following the industrial revolution of the early twentieth century and again following World War II that, in each case, led to more prosperity for the middle and working classes.

Until then, the organization—regardless of tax status—must sub-scribe to a model of ethical financial stability on behalf of its stakehold-ers by embracing a reasonable dose of international, federal, state, local, and industry regulations. The prosperous organization will prevail by hiring, training, monitoring, and motivating quality teams and individ-uals that play the game the right way.

Customer Satisfaction is the Ultimate Report Card

Successful new customer acquisition; quality products and services; col-lecting receivables with diligence; practicing dynamic regulatory com-pliance; and improved financial stability are relegated to mere academic fodder for the organization if substantial customer contentment is not present.

Teams and individuals of distinction embrace customer satisfaction as the *ultimate report card*. Without motivated buyers of its goods or services, the organization is no longer playing with a full deck dealt at its inception and has stopped playing the game the right way.

An organization of distinction's ultimate success lies in its cus-tomers' thorough and consistent measurement of happiness. When de-prived of satisfied customers, all other metrics become meaningless.

Treat customer satisfaction as your ultimate report card of success. You are guaranteed to prevail in all five of the other cultural realities; and forever maintain an organization, team, or career of distinction in the transformational workplace.

Individuals Playing as One Cohesive Team

In its simplest form, baseball involves a group of statistics-driven individual athletes finding ways to play as a team to win games and championships. This dynamic is no different for any team, regardless of industry.

Stakeholders within the organization are measured for individual performance, although each must play the game the right way by working together as a cohesive team. By driving sales, financing customers, developing and delivering quality and relevant products and services, collecting receivables, managing regulations and industry standards, providing robust financial results, and producing satisfied customers, the team—as well as its members—have the opportunity to win the game.

The new standard in the twenty-first-century workplace is to play the game with passion and the will to win, coupled with a renewed noble purpose and lifelong commitment to sustainable products and services resulting in workforce development and socioeconomic ascension in the greater public interest.

Five

Leadership and Teamwork by Inclusion

S uccessful organizations balance seven interested stakeholders. Teams of distinction generate critical tactical and strategic decisions based on what is best for the organization and its primary participants. The practice of leadership or teamwork that includes all relevant stakeholders in crucial decision-making more often yields organizations, teams, and individual careers of distinction.

The Seven Principal Stakeholders of Thriving Organizations:

- Customers - the paying clientele and lifelong ambassadors.
- Employees - the team members that produce products and services and support customers.
- Ownership - the shareholders, donors, or taxpayers that provide needed capital infusion.
- Corporate or administration - that operates the organization on behalf of the ownership.
- Vendors - that provide essential operational products or services.
- Competitors - that prevent the organization from becoming complacent or predatory.
- Community - including legislators, regulators, accreditors, industry observers, and independent board members or advisors who oversee the organization's public interest.

Does the Customer Always Come First?

A long-standing cross-industry decree says that the customer always comes first. However, such doctrines are negotiable if situations dictate that the customers may benefit by putting other stakeholders foremost.

A typical example is a new regulation or standard that is unpopular with consumers yet not negotiable. Implement by explaining to your clients the *why* behind the action without throwing the third-party overseer under the bus. Because in the eyes of customers and other stakeholders, comprehending the why behind a decision often reverses the initial non-acceptance. Although disapproving of the verdict, many will concede to an acceptable level of understanding.

Whether at the organization, team, or individual level, it is good practice to contemplate the benefits and possible consequences to the seven principal stakeholders when making significant decisions, developing strategic plans, designing products or services, or crafting mission statements. And it is advisable to include other relevant stakeholders unique to your organization, where and when practical, before reaching final decisions or implementing new strategies.

In nonprofit and public service organizations, processes sometimes have built-in mechanisms that trigger required stakeholder input, often referred to as *shared governance*. Similar horizontal approaches to hierarchy are practiced less within the for-profit business model, although incorporating customers and other stakeholders into vertical decision lines may produce an equal perception of inclusion; and thereby contribute to a harmonious and productive workplace.

Distinctive Organizations Respect Everyone's Career

Whether a customer, colleague, owner, shareholder, donor, taxpayer, corporate staffer, senior manager, vendor; competitor, legislator, regulator, an industry observer, accreditor, independent board member, or adviser, hold the career of every stakeholder in high regard by joining in a commitment to partnership.

Implement the following paradigm into your organization or team's culture, and I guarantee it harvests improvement of stakeholder retention and gratification never thought possible:

- Every day, give your customers a reason to come back tomorrow.
- Every day, give each other a reason to come back tomorrow.

Contemplate redesigning your operational model to acknowledge the existence and respect the organization's seven principal stakeholders' needs. Rest assured each will be grateful for the deliberate inclusion.

Develop Compelling Strategies

Mission statements are often required by an organization's articles of incorporation or charter, if not by accreditation or other industry standards. Proclamations of the vision and core values of the enterprise are also a good practice. Although the right persons, including interested stakeholders, are required to develop strategies that transform and sustain your organization as a great place to learn, earn, and grow.

When implementing a new strategy, practice good leadership, revising the mission statement, or declaring a renewed vision or core value by supporting product development, customer service, regulatory compliance, stakeholder inclusion, and appropriate celebrations of victories.

Stakeholder Inclusive Strategic Initiatives:

- Commit to offering external professional development as a benefit, not a privilege.
- Foster customer loyalty with intensive product training and support services.
- Sponsor a legitimate internal staff development program.

- Cultivate branded partnerships and promote them in the community.
- Hold vendors accountable, but treat each as a valued stakeholder.
- Drive and reward a culture of compliance, integrity, and ethics.
- Celebrate success, often and in public, for customers and other stakeholders.
- Schedule regular staff meetings with approved awards at each level:
  - Ownership
  - Administration
  - Department
  - Staff

Any holistic approach to strategic development that embraces and rewards participation from each of the seven stakeholders is a critical step toward building an organization, team, or career of distinction.

Define Your Economic Driver

Because of the public's general dissonance toward making a profit or surplus at the struggling consumer's expense, an unintended consequence is disregarding the interconnected economic model. An organization's economic model drives the mutually dependent bottom lines of positive customer outcomes and profitability or financial stability.

Mutually Dependent Bottom Lines:

- The customer is seeking consummation of needs or wants.
- The organization is pursuing customer satisfaction toward sustainable profitability or financial surplus.

In many organizations—whether for-profit, nonprofit or in the public service—one bottom line cannot be obtained ethically without the other. When customers are satisfied with the acquired product or service, the organization often experiences an increase in profits or surplus, assuming sound fiscal management. And by reinvesting a reasonable portion of the profits or surplus back into the operation's capital structure, more customers may have the opportunity to benefit from the product or service offered.

Although counterintuitive in its dynamic, such mutual dependence of outcomes and profitability is a valuable starting point in defining or redefining your organization's economic engine. In today's challenging regulatory and competitive climates, it may be necessary to ramp up the motor by adding several additional cylinders as appropriate.

Strong sales potential is not an excuse to ignore suitable capital availability levels, projected customer demand, and potential profit or surplus. Regulatory compliance, combined with the product or service's forecasted market share, capital requirements, and qualified staff's availability to develop, market, and deliver the product or service, is paramount to its holistic, sustainable success.

Stop Making Chicken

How often do organizations "make chicken," an operational tactic in the fast-food business, where a new menu item is rolled out in haste because the restaurant across the street started offering it?

Organizations in other industries or sectors make chicken by introducing new products or services born of limited feasibility based on sales potential, competitive threats, or market demand. These goods or services are produced lightning fast with template-driven corporate, state, accreditation, federal, and international approval applications, as required. The results are new product offerings that attract scores of customers with limited satisfaction or just as frustrating, favorable customer approval ratings, yet minimal sales volume.

In today's competitive, regulation-saturated workplaces, an organization, more than ever, needs to rebuild its economic engine by encompassing key drivers necessary for maintaining popular and sustainable products and services.

Ponder this sample product or service-specific mission statement:

> Predictable sales potential supported by real-time outcomes assessment or comprehensive feasibility that demonstrate the product or service is approval worthy, has an affordable cost structure, sufficient staffing capability, acceptable levels of customer satisfaction, substantial market demand, full regulatory compliance, and adequate capital investment.

Mission integrity is crucial. Any new or mature product or service failing to deliver pre-determined qualifiers measured with minimal organizational, team, regulatory, and industry standards is a candidate to divest; or is denied at the planning stage owing to insufficient feasibility.

Define your economic driver, write it down, and then broadcast it for organizational, team, and individual buy-in, as well as soliciting suggestions for continuous improvement.

Quality Begets Quantity

It is perhaps the organization's responsibility—in the interest of the seven principal stakeholders—to offer goods and services that produce targeted quantity through quality instead of the more common inverse approach of favoring quantity. Selling widgets or amenities and then practicing crisis intervention to overcome higher than expected market demand or difficult-to-reach customer outcomes is a fool's game in today's competitive local and global marketplaces.

Failed practices by overzealous practitioners that reasoned quantity invoked quality fill organizational graveyards. I submit these resting places of commerce's worse days, perhaps are becoming overshot with uncut grass and wilted flowers. Indeed, a welcomed reprieve allowing the organization's seven deserved stakeholders an opportunity to be active, valued players in the workforce development and subsequent socioeconomic improvement of the twenty-first century.

Six

Make Your Workplace a Great Place

In the unending quest to play the game the right way, teams or individuals adhere to a defined set of rules that apply to specific organizations and industries. I have uncovered a handful of simple rules common to many sectors that go far in setting a culture of distinction, i.e., by transforming the workplace into a great place. Indeed, each may be modified to fit the unique aspects of any organization, team, or individual career.

Hello Zones

How often do you pass a customer, colleague, or visitor in the office building, shop, store, factory, warehouse, clinic, or field, only to find that person looking down or away? In high school, you may have succumbed to insecurities in a similar moment and concluded you were unworthy. Similar interaction in the adult world of work is often a sign the passerby is the individual that is lacking confidence or self-esteem. Therefore, it is an inherited obligation for the organization's stakeholders to transform common areas into *hello zones*.

Hello zones inspire workplace culture by requiring employees to acknowledge those with whom paths cross, regardless of whether they are customers, colleagues, or visitors. Simple eye contact—accompanied by a warm and enthusiastic hello—inspires the unassuming partner to raise their head and return the gesture. Should the person be already known, expand the hello zone by engaging with appropriate comments or questions based on an established mutual understanding.

I implemented hello zones at several inherited operations and was thrilled by the positive energy levels developed in the common work areas. It may seem contrived when first shared with a new employee during orientation, although I have never heard a single complaint about the hello zones.

If not already practicing this cultural wake-up protocol, begin today. You may be amazed at the results, including a work environment of increased morale and improved customer satisfaction. Operate hello zones and experience the joy of work. Active hello zones are a testament to the dedicated work of ownership, staff, vendors, and other internal stakeholders. Hello zones support those efforts. Hello zones work.

Workplace Safety and Security

Does your workplace require photo identification for on-site employees? A mandatory sign-in and pass procedure for visitors? How about security personnel equipped with video software to monitor the comings and goings during hours of operation? Does your workplace maintain a camera and motion security system with central monitoring during off-hours? How about a safety or security committee that convenes per a regular timetable?

To be sure, international, federal, state, or local government regulations trigger some security measures. Nonetheless, I was once confronted by two separate and stark reminders, in a single day, on why a safe and secure workplace is as important as quality control and financially stable operations.

On the morning of April 16, 2007, I was in my office serving as campus president of a prominent career training school when I saw the tragic news flash on the internet that gunfire had killed thirty-two persons and wounded seventeen others at Virginia Polytechnic Institute and State University, also known as Virginia Tech. The perpetrator was a lone gunman, a senior student at the university with a mental illness history.

Later that morning, a dental assistant program student entered my office inquiring about our campus security procedures. I responded with empathy, expressing the horror of the Virginia Tech shootings, that I understood her concerns, and assured her the school acts out of safety first for our students, faculty, and staff. She looked confused as she responded, "Oh my god, I had no idea, that is horrible, but the reason for my visit is I was just in the student lounge buying something from a vending machine when I felt a tap on my shoulder. I turned around, and it was my ex-boyfriend." He was not a student at the school.

Startled by this correlated and shocking concern, I sprang from my seat and assisted the student in her time of need. Everything worked out okay as her ex-boyfriend left with no incident.

Buoyed with a renewed sense of urgency, I convened the campus safety and security committee to implement unprecedented measures. The updated plan included photo identification for students and employees; a sign-in/sign-out procedure for visitors, including vendors; uniformed security personnel at open-access entrances; online video surveillance; and an electronic fob system where those sanctioned with coded keys opened the exterior doors of the building. The same exterior doors opened unencumbered from the inside to facilitate emergency exiting.

Although most of these new security measures were unbudgeted, there was no objection from a just as concerned corporate office.

Several months later, an epilogue to this story occurred when I obtained a well-written nineteen-page manual courtesy of Virginia Tech titled, *How to Respond to Disruptive or Threatening Student Behavior.* The informative report's tragic irony is the University published it two years before the horrific mass shooting.

In many workplaces, retail establishments, notwithstanding, we are fortunate to operate in a closed society instead of the open environments of traditional college campuses such as Virginia Tech. I had reminded faculty and staff about our willingness and ability to remove an unstable student or employee from the school long before he or she became a severe threat to our well-being. Upgrading our campus safety and security, post-Virginia Tech, was our responsibility as well, as we inherited a newfound commitment not to take anything for granted.

Having occurred two years after the university wrote a manual for dealing with troubled students, the Virginia Tech shooting provokes the twofold importance of 1) having a plan and 2) working the plan. The tragedy further reminds us that well-intentioned programs are vulnerable. Regardless, it is another blunt reminder that your organization must have a comprehensive security blueprint in place.

Please do it for your customers, employees, and visitors, and in memory and honor of the forty-nine victims and their families, friends, and colleagues at Virginia Tech.

Lights On

When visiting a retail store during regular hours of operation, it is rare to encounter a department with its lights turned off. Nonetheless, why is it common to see the lights off in some areas of other physical workplace operations during regular business or office hours? I am a proponent of energy conservation for environmental and financial reasons, but customers, employees, and visitors deserve a well-lit, open-for-business environment.

The *lights-on* rule is sympathetic to employees, customers, or other visitors that often enter a building, shop, or store of vacated offices, labs, departments, and common areas, some darkened from the learned habit of turning lights off and closing the door behind. To supersede such a tendency, implement a rule of thumb where those approved to open and close the workplace each day have exclusive control of the lighting.

Walk Directions

When a customer, new employee, or visitor asks for directions to a department, office, or bathroom, walk him or her to the destination as opposed to offering the confusing:

> "Go down there and make your second right into the hallway, then make a left, and the department you are looking for is the third door on the right. To be sure, check the door plaque to confirm you are in the right place before you enter."

The above example is an exaggeration, yet if left to navigate alone, rest assured the customer, employee, or visitor is again asking for directions on the way. Walk the person or group to the destination and use the journey as an opportunity for a productive conversation. Everyone will feel better because of the extra effort. Make walking directions a workplace-wide rule. Stakeholder value points are guaranteed to tick up on surveys from this act of genuine customer service.

Walk directions is a rule common to physical ground workplaces. However, it may be tailored to virtual online or call center operations by providing electronic instructions upon the site visitor or caller's request. Integrate follow-up mechanisms to track customer progress.

Regardless of the platform, remember to walk, not talk, directions.

Return Customer Inquiries Within 24 Hours

Virtual interaction with customers has taken many forms in the information age: voice mail, texts, emails, online forums, website inquiries, social media, and other electronic vehicles. A mandatory twenty-four-hour return message rule creates urgency. Better yet, make it the same day or same hour, or same minute for that matter bearing in mind to-day's instantaneous world created by the internet and smartphones.

I led a sales team that each evening and weekend sent a company-owned smartphone home with an anointed representative to respond in real-time to online inquiries. Technology providers now market smart-phones with interactive software for a more systematic approach to electronic customer communication.

Perhaps the day is near where each department in an organization is armed with smartphones loaded with intelligent apps to ensure prompt communication at each level of the customer timeline, assuming that twenty-four-hour call or data centers do not exist for practical reasons. An off-hour smartphone response strategy makes good technical sense as a renewed competitive edge. At a minimum, it projects customer service savvy in the rapid-response world of the sharing economy.

Automatic replies generated during off-hours have become compulsory, although each inquiry needs to be returned by a human at some point. And automatic responses should never substitute a live person or personal message in real-time during regular business hours.

Regardless of the customer's electronic vehicle, and in the absence of a call or data center, return the inquiry within twenty-four hours, or better yet, in a New York minute.

Be Wary of Airing Dirty Laundry

In the sensitive to privacy world of today, it is an obligation to be cognizant of what you share in public, thereby requiring an astute sense of space in the workplace as worthwhile discussions about customers and coworkers are common between staff.

Contemplate implementing training guidance of looking over both shoulders, closing the door if appropriate, and being conscious of who is in earshot before embarking on an important—and legal— conversation for the benefit of the customer or colleague in focus. Organizations that are privacy-sensitive remind all stakeholders to practice earshot maintenance before engaging in an appropriate discussion with others.

A magnificent characteristic of organizations and teams of distinction is how employees act in the office, clinic, factory, warehouse, hallway, parking lot, field, call center, or online platform often correlates to the customer and worker happiness levels. Thus, partner to service well and lead by example.

Under Promise, Then Over Deliver

At the career training institutions that I led, I made a habit of asking student customers about his or her overall experience and how the current course or student service was progressing. The answer often was, "It is better than I thought it was going to be." A welcomed reminder that faculty and staff were promising the student enough to remain motivated without being set up for later disappointment.

Whether participating in customer engagement or employee relations, search for ways to under-promise, thus allowing your colleagues to over-deliver the product or service. It is an art requiring training and practice that is guaranteed to pay dividends in customer satisfaction and employee morale.

Your colleagues will appreciate your modest contribution of under-promising, thereby permitting him or her to over-deliver the product or service. Corporate or administrative personnel and regulators or accreditors appreciate organizations that practice this rule as part of an ethical workplace. On a conscious level, customers may not be aware of being underpromised and over-delivered the product or services, although they may sense something positive is happening.

Transform Your Customers to Raving Fans

If the definition of *good* customer service is going above and beyond to assist a client, then the meaning of *excellent* customer service is:

> Going above and beyond for the customer with *genuine enjoyment.*

I often agree with colleagues in customer-driven professions that such work is not suitable for the faint of heart. As discussed in Chapter Two: Build an Organization, Team, or Career of Distinction, assertive, self-motivated, and customer-intensive professionals with a strong work ethic are often the most successful workplace performers. Although a genuine approach to customer service is crucial to this simple rule for making your workplace a great place:

> Transform customers to *raving fans* of your products and services.

When assisting customers—whether in buying, financing, learning, improving, donating, or participating—is performed without intentional care and empathy, customer relations, regardless of field, indeed becomes a stressful and challenging job.

You engage in real-time with your customers on behalf of your team and organization. Genuine enjoyment of the experience—whether a good day or a bad day for the employee or customer—is a foundation for lifelong success in an individual's career. Love it or leave it as the saying goes, although choosing to stay should be inspired by an appreciation for your chosen occupation and your organization or team's culture. You are changing lives for the better, including your own.

But customer service and employee relations are more than just being polite. Maintaining professionalism is expected, although empathy often outdoes sympathy.

For example, as a new director of student admissions at a career college, I once met with a prospective student on behalf of an admissions representative because the aspiring student had enrolled and then canceled her application for the third time without completing the financial aid and orientation processes. I had a frank conversation with the applicant about how not following through was likely affecting her entire life. And although I understood her fear of the tuition financing process and what could go wrong with eligibility, in general, to cancel without the details amounted to self-sabotage on her part.

The prospective student proceeded to become defensive, accusing me of being interested in her starting school because that was my job. I responded by sharing that I already had a career, thus, the conversation was not about me but her obtaining a meaningful job. And I meant every word of it. At that point, she left my office without saying goodbye and proceeded out of the building.

I informed the admissions representative that I was not successful in saving her potential student customer.

Several minutes later, as I was looking down at my desk, I felt a presence in front of me. When I looked up, lo and behold, it was the same prospective student. She shared that she sat in her car thinking about our discussion and was habitually adverse to follow through. She volunteered that I was the first person ever to confront her about these fears and how she was letting them stop her from pursuing the dream of an honorable career, not to mention its adverse effect on other aspects of her life.

In the end, she scheduled a financial aid appointment, attended orientation, started school, graduated, and was placed in a full-time position by the career services team. I had been fortunate to learn earlier in my career that empathy and genuine customer service drive successful teams and organizations. And as the new director of student admissions at that particular campus, conveying an excellent first impression on the team that day was a bonus. Although, in my mind, what mattered most is the student customer was the clear winner from the honest interaction.

Practice What You Preach and Teach

Practicing what we preach and teach in the presence of customers and colleagues are expected behaviors from stakeholders in any organization.

Whether in the office, shop, store, factory, warehouse, clinic, or field, having well-defined employees' rules is paramount to an effective product or service delivery toward improved employee morale and positive customer outcomes. On the contrary, in employees' eyes, published declarations in human resource manuals and policy handbooks become meaningless if influential stakeholders violate similar pronouncements.

Here is a shortlist of traditions practiced by ethical stakeholders at organizations that are playing the game the right way:

Highly Effective Habits Found at Great Workplaces:

- Good attendance
- On-time performance
- Positive attitude
- Professional appearance
- Coordinated work area
- Cleanliness and hygiene
- Teamwork and collaboration
- Ethical service
- Lifelong learning

Forever remain on your toes after setting ground rules for your organization or team. You may be flatfooted when called out for behavior to the contrary. Practice what you preach and teach for a harmonious and productive organization, team, or individual career of distinction.

Produce and Finance a Sunshine Committee

Any organization or team committed to employee welfare may consider sponsoring a *Sunshine Committee* to ensure that colleagues are acknowledged for both personal and professional achievements such as:

- Birthdays
- Work anniversaries
- Successful project completion
- Community involvement
- Awards and special commendations
- Going above and beyond the call of duty

To be effective, the Sunshine Committee should be budgeted and staffed by volunteers permitted to conduct group activities during regular business hours. Employee privacy must be assured by having each sign-off on what may or may not be broadcasted or celebrated by the committee.

Initiate, fund, staff, and manage equitable employee celebrations via a Sunshine Committee or equivalent, and I guarantee employee morale reaches levels never thought attainable.

Make Your Workplace a Great Place to Work

Developing and administering a clear set of simple rules for organizational or team constituents to adhere to is essential in an outcomes-focused, open atmosphere workplace. Employees are thankful for tidy workspaces; customers for product and service consistency; vendors for appropriate use of its ancillary goods and services; and government regulators and industry accreditors for the devotion to compliance produced as a result.

Nevertheless, some personalities do oppose anything labeled a rule. Call it something else when deemed necessary by the organizational or team culture. In the spirit of practicing effective leadership or team-work, perhaps name it "the art of fairness and inclusion."

However labeled, implement or follow simple rules—albeit practical, affordable, and enjoyable—and make your workplace a great place to learn, earn, and grow.

Seven

Your Essential Role in the Transformational Workplace

Perhaps it goes without saying that the local and global workplaces are evolving and, one may argue, not always in a positive direction. We have transitioned from the supervisor/worker-centered dynamic of the twentieth century to the early twenty-first century owner/employer/investor/donor-centered workplace. Nonetheless, unfair organizational models dominated by a few at the top have a limited chance of surviving the now internet-enabled global awareness of the masses. Extremism notwithstanding, the 2016 U.S. presidential primary campaigns reminded us that societal power is returning to "we the people," regardless of the candidates' political ideologue or social appropriateness.

With almost absolute conviction, similar populism is on the verge of transcending to the workplace with a mission toward the long-awaited normalcy of gender equality, fair wages, and horizontal organizational charts. This transition from the latter half of the last century's norm of worker containment to the twenty-first century's burgeoning workplace of people-driven transformation appears imminent.

In the wake of the epic policy-driven build-up of the wealthiest "one percent" from about 1982 to 2007, we are now facing a historical repeat of the early twentieth century. During that time, worker and policy revolts against the famed Robber Barons of the industrial revolution—Vanderbilt, Rockefeller, Carnegie, and J.P. Morgan, to name a few—were front-page news. Today, the global information revolution and the Great Recession's failure to correct the excess at the top has further buoyed the current socioeconomic phenomenon, once again at the expense of the middle and working classes.

Granted, the unionization or regulatory actions on the Robber Barons era's working conditions appear not to be driving today's transformation. Perhaps the twenty-first century workers will experience equal rights laws and tax policies that benefit all Americans, not just a select few that are "lucky enough to be born with the long straw," as lamented by famous billionaire investor Warren Buffett.

The rapid diversification of racial makeup and sexual identity in the twenty-first century's general population may overpower any resistance from the new minority at the top. The last time workers in the U.S. middle classes were worthy participants in the economy—i.e., enjoyed prosperity with manageable debt levels—was the post-World War II era when the federal government taxed the wealthiest citizens at 91% of earned income.

As a result of this income tax policy, several massive U.S. government initiatives at the time were financed with little or no sustained federal deficits. The Marshall Plan and other grants cleaned up Europe and Japan following World War II. U.S. involvement in the Korean War of the early 1950s. Escalation of the Cold War and construction of the interstate highway system in the same decade. Plus, the Vietnam War—coupled with the historic Apollo moon shot—of the 1960s.

Social acceptance notwithstanding, each of these developments created jobs that led to unprecedented prosperity for America's middle and working classes during that time. I remember a discussion in my undergraduate macroeconomics class where we theorized that the Vietnam War and the American economy both peaked in 1967, and the parallel was not a coincidence.

To be sure, excessive taxation—or controversial wars—by any means are not the answer, although neither was the other extreme of the 1980s and early 2000s when the U.S. lowered tax rates on its wealthiest citizens in anticipation of trickle-down job creation. And we all know where those reverse taxation policies led: the non-exponential growth of the top one percent of wealth at the expense of ballooning federal deficits and flat job and income growth for the middle and working classes in America.

Nonetheless, beyond placing our vote on Election Day, government regulation and tax policies are, for the most part, out of our control. Nevertheless, we are accountable for our workplace and its professional and financial influences on ourselves and fellow stakeholders' careers and lives.

What is your essential role in the transformational workplace of the twenty-first century? Contemplate the following models that speak to progressive workplace reinvention.

The Millennial Model

My personal career experience centered on fellow Baby Boomers—a generation that, in general, was born between 1946 and 1964—and Generation X, or those born between about 1965 and 1977. For the most part, I enjoyed a shared, productive work ethic with these two demographic groups.

Following initial discomfort, I have come to admire the renewed work ethic of the so-called Y and Millennial generations, or those current workplace-aged adults born between about 1978 and 1995. From a general viewpoint, this youngest workplace cohort appears to champion the following model (hypothetical Y or Millennial person speaking):

- I prefer casual work attire but formal communications equipment.
- Blending my job and personal lives into the same existence is natural for me and in contrast to the Baby Boomer and X generations' tendency to separate work and private lives.
- Show me a horizontal leadership hierarchy because I also want to experience you as a coworker, not just as a boss.

- My parents are my most trusted friends, and I expect my boss to be a good friend as well.
- Whenever necessary, I shall promote myself by moving onward and upward at another organization instead of climbing the previous ladder to the proverbial glass ceiling.
- Yes, I do deserve a trophy (workplace translation - a paycheck) just for showing up. That is half the battle.
- Equal pay for equal work—regardless of race or gender—needs to be the law of the land.
- Livable wages are a right, not a privilege.
- I do not despise the 'one percent' as I aspire to become an exclusive club member.
- When acting unethically, one-percenters must be held accountable and not bailed out by the taxpayers.
- A college-level education is now the equivalent of high school education for previous generations. Thus, a college degree needs to be affordable for anyone willing and able to pursue one.
- A fun, innovative, productive, and flexible workplace is a great place to work.

Despite inherent faults from being designed for the masses by an emerging cohort generation, the Millennial Model deserves serious thought as this century's evolving workplace culture. These ethical, refreshing, and equitable dictums create a profound argument for regulated or fair market capitalism in tomorrow's diverse demographic global workplace. Not to mention Millennials, by population default, will soon dominate the workforce.

Just as clean air and water, our children and grandchildren deserve a place of work inclusive of diversity and equality in the pursuit of corporate profits or nonprofit surpluses. The Millennial Model may accomplish in this century what the Boomer and X generations perhaps exploited or avoided in the previous era.

The Expert Economy

During my thirty-plus years in the workplace, I have witnessed a transformation that went from an employee servant to the intrapreneur, i.e., an employed entrepreneur, to the present-day independent contractor or mobile employee that offers expertise to the highest or most convenient bidder.

It is often studied and written that independent contracting of the transitional and flexible worker—Internal Revenue Service concerns of this so-called *gig economy* notwithstanding—may become the norm in the twenty-first-century workplace.

I imagine the Internet's pending upgrade to the more personalized Web 3.0 will transform telecommuting to standard practice instead of the present exception. Nevertheless, the Millennials' migrations to urban centers and traditional workplaces may persist in the near term.

Occupational expertise—whether academic, scientific, creative, or skilled; and whether practiced at the traditional workplace or virtually from home—may continue to set the tone for worker viability in the twenty-first century's local and global marketplaces.

Lifelong Learning

Lifelong learning has become paramount to success in both professional and personal pursuits. How are you meeting the continuing education requirements of your profession or occupation in the next qualifying year? What are your long-term goals regarding first or advanced college degree attainment?

The transformational workplace's human resource policies may need to honor alternative education pursuits toward job and career improvement. To remain competitive in attracting and retaining elite talent, corporations, nonprofits, and public agencies cannot ignore online learning proliferation. The flexibility and convenience provided to the employee by this viable academic delivery model are substantial.

Of course, the student loan debt crisis needs to correct or be reversed for individual careers of distinction to flourish in this century. Perhaps a move away from student loan intensive education programs toward cost-effective skills training may drive the needed further reinvention of academic delivery models. Coding camps and similar short-term and often online prototypes are setting this trend of expert career training.

Regardless, the quest for learning should be an ongoing tradition of life. Solon, the Greek philosopher, perhaps said it best:

> *Grow older learning something new every day.*

Career Development

Social science experts may forever debate how skill, ambition, personality, and luck influence career achievement. Just as important is how an individual defines their measurements of success. Money as a yardstick? Making a difference? Providing for loved ones? Excellent benefits package? Contributing as part of a team? Being on a mission of purpose? Perhaps all of the above, and more?

Your role in the twenty-first-century workplace predisposes a challenge to think about what is essential to your career, an activity we perhaps spend half of our waking life pursuing.

In today's dog eat dog world of work, some employees and business owners are reexamining the time and energy invested in the workplace relating to the return on investment of income and self-fulfillment. He or she may feel held hostage from the pursuit of a work/life balance. Other workers are content, whereas the career-centered may deem their occupation as the defining aspect of life. This career commitment level is evident in a typical *New York Times* obituary, where professional achievements often dominate the headline and copy.

Find common ground by using your career compass to establish a clear perspective of what is important to you in your professional life and how it affects other areas of your being.

Here is the doctrine I follow within the career domain of life:

> Discover what you enjoy, then make every effort to be the best in the world at it, thus allowing you the opportunity to make a living doing it.

Whether an employee, business owner, volunteer or home-maker—perhaps all four—or seeking employment, the commitment to career development provides an excellent opportunity to write down what you believe is your professional mission, now and in the future. For twenty-five years running, mine is:

" *Making a living by making a difference.* "

What is your career mission statement? Keep it simple, make it smart, and write it down.

Compensation

Did you know that everyone earns the same amount of money? I call it *not enough*. Money is primarily generated by our careers yet is personal in nature. Nevertheless, it is wise to leave emotions out of your compensation management and set career goals with purpose.

Take responsibility for stretching your presumed competitive compensation by eliminating a credit card balance, and reach further out for higher aspirations such as paying off that onerous student loan. Treat personal financial management as a business at home, and you are more apt to prevail in the compensation wars at work.

As far as making more of it, reflect on the principle of first doing what you enjoy or possess a natural talent in, and then becoming the best possible at your chosen occupation. The money may follow your passion.

Work/Life Balance

In today's hurried world, work/life balance continues as a hot topic. I submit that individuals have the ultimate control over balancing his or her professional and personal domains. We may blame our boss, employer, or financial burdens for generating too much work and not enough play. However, we must take responsibility for the final decision on best using our most limited resource: time.

Planning for improved work/life balance is a fabulous place to start by setting short and long term goals toward spending more time doing things you enjoy, whether it is traveling, video gaming, following your favorite sports, fishing, antique shopping, reading, skiing, or hiking a nature trail. The list of potential leisure activities may far exceed what we accomplish at our jobs.

There is no excuse for neglecting to design a work/life balance plan if that is important to you. To survive in the workplace, we often need to live a holistic life of equilibrium.

Pursue the free time activities and hobbies that interest you. Some of the finer moments in our lives occur outside of the workplace.

Giving Back

Karma sometimes dictates that *we get what we give*. For some, giving back is a fundamental domain of life's purpose. Whether volunteering for a local charity; or providing a community service by offering your time, pro bono, such as a baseball coach, Girl Scouts troop leader, or a nonprofit board member, the near and long term possibilities are endless in community activism.

Transferring your education and workplace acquired skill sets may create significant, lifelong contributions to your community, country, or the world. For those searching for ways to give back, think of your workplace contributions as a starting point. I guarantee you discover resourceful opportunities that may lead to a fulfilling role of charitable service in your community or beyond.

In today's challenging world—inhabited by the haves and have-nots—boundless opportunities exist to contribute, such as volunteering or donating to charitable organizations. The Internal Revenue Service acknowledges select charitable donations as deductible on your income tax return, thus adding potential support to your money domain. Consult a professional tax advisor for details.

And remember to give back to your workplace or career by acting as a mentor to up-and-coming talent so that he or she may benefit from the wisdom of your experience and expertise. It is a professional obligation where you may learn more than you teach.

Giving back to your community and workplace are great ways to set profound, achievable goals each year that may improve your job or business performance as well.

The Workplace is Your Place

Your essential role in the transformational workplace of tomorrow is first to take emotional and intellectual ownership of your stake in the business, organization, or team that employs you today.

Be a champion of the workable status quo, all the while promoting necessary change instead of the more customary anti-stakeholder rants that accomplish little. The rank and file need to retake possession of their place of employment using new and ethical approaches.

Unionization saved the worker of the early twentieth century. However, with some notable exceptions, the collective bargaining movement has experienced a slow and steady decline as an institution, perhaps because of greed, mismanagement, or illegal activities.

Today's prominent unions—assuming survival by ethical and law-abiding practices—seem to represent more of the affluent and privileged, such as film and television actors, commercial pilots, college professors, and professional athletes. Thus, what gives for the rest of us?

Perhaps populist movements that are professional and constructive may garner employers' attention that does not feel as threatened as it might otherwise to the collective bargaining of impending unionization under current labor laws, assuming adherence to the rules exists. Indeed, openness to communication from the organization's leaders precipitates any crusade to make changes by loyal members of the team in question. But a collaborative approach to workplace effectiveness may need horizontal hierarchies and other potential transformations as exhibited within the Millennial Model.

Job security remains a fragile component of today's workplace; therefore, tread with care when inspiring colleague-supported actions toward necessary organizational change. Nonetheless, be a player as opposed to a spectator.

* * *

That written, the present struggles of the American—and perhaps global—workplaces remain noteworthy. Regardless of products or services offered, measure an organization's intrinsic value toward building teams and individual careers of distinction by its willingness to put people first.

Favor the organization that hires or refers colleagues for their optimism; then trains for quality, monitors for compliance, and motivates for performance. Create or be part of an organization that includes relevant stakeholders in critical decision-making, follows a prescribed set of simple rules for everyday workplace success, and always plays the game the right way.

Regardless of your position or rank, remember to stand up and be counted—as the worthy participant that you are—by taking ownership of your essential role in the transformational workplace. Be the ethical stakeholder that leads or supports the ascension of your workplace to a great place. And forever enjoy a prosperous career of distinction.

NOTES

[1]*GOOD TO GREAT – Why Some Companies Make the Leap...and Others Don't*. Copyright © 2001 by Jim Collins. Published by Harper Business (an imprint of HarperCollins Publishers, Inc.) For more information, visit jim-collins.com. Reprinted with permission of Curtis Brown, Ltd.

David J. Waldron is an individual investor and the author of self-improvement books for those seeking to achieve the personal and professional goals that matter most in their life.

In addition to *Hire Train Monitor Motivate*, David has written three other nonfiction books. His latest release, *Build Wealth with Common Stocks*, was written for individual investors seeking to fund life's significant milestones. *The Ten Domains of Effective Goal Setting* provides the reader with a practical template for achieving goals in life's essential areas. *A Great Place to Learn & Earn* is David's professional memoir as a former 25-year veteran of postsecondary career education.

He is working with his wife, Suzan, on her memoir, *One of a Million Faces*, about living and coping with Type 1 diabetes and its complications.

David earned a Bachelor of Science in business studies as a Garden State Scholar at Stockton University and completed The Practice of Management Program at Brown University. He and Suzan reside in historic South Central Pennsylvania, USA.

Take control and achieve your dreams at davidjwaldron.com.

www.ingramcontent.com/pod-product-compliance
Lightning Source LLC
Chambersburg PA
CBHW031539040426
42445CB00010B/618